Praise for
Get Stuck on Happy

Easy read which is a difficult task to achieve. Congrats! Love the vibration cards, very catchy and powerful to change your vibration. Thank you for the kind mention. It is very humbling to have had the opportunity to come into your life at the right time and make a positive impact.   — Devlyn Steele

I love that this book is short and simple and that the ideas are written in a "want this... then practice this" form. You have reinvented the present day's teachings of the "New Testament" in a pocketbook!   — Barb Sim

Janet Legere's latest book is a must-read. Extremely well-written. Lots of suggestions and links to put anyone's mind in a happier place. The book reflects Janet's personality, her kindness and willingness to help others.   — Maureen Charlton

I so enjoyed reading and reflecting on your passion for such a needed and underrated "commodity". You send your message out with joy and enthusiasm, sharing selflessly with all ... Nice work.
— Pam Comstock

This book is a fantastic attempt to bring Janet's light to your world. I strongly urge you to read this book all the way through once and reflect on the simplicity of her heartfelt gift to you. When you read it the second time, stop and use the tools she has acquired through years of experience as a real person using the education of life to help you find your happy. I cannot say enough about how thrilled I am you got your hands on this book. Janet will help you find the most important thing in life ... happiness. — Will Buckley

Janet has written her 30 ways to be happy in a very thorough and productive manner that will help anyone that would love to be more happy on a daily basis... I have and still use these 30 steps and have become a much more loving person and feel I can accomplish anything! I highly recommend this book to everyone! Anyone can benefit immensely by following these 30 steps to being happy. Be prepared to start living a happier life. — Claudia Adcock

This book is everything it promises to be. If you put her advice into practice, you will absolutely, without fail, be a happier person for it, and your family will be too. — Laura Vero-Augustine

Bravo. Janet's secret ingredients to happiness have finally been revealed. Her daily positive thoughts and attitude are truly contagious and inspiring. You always leave her company happier than when you arrived. Now we can all be that happy person you want to meet. — Tammy Holt-Cote

I read *Get Stuck On Happy* yesterday and... Today it inspired me to write a Happy Card. It reads: Make Someone Laugh today. I followed that with some deep breathing before plunging into a day of work ... I love this book which is thoughtful and lays out a wonderful path to a creative, a life full of joy. — Jane Mark

You are holding in your hands a simple, yet powerful road map to happiness. Janet has created that map based on her own journey and her years of helping others in business and in their personal lives. I can tell you, if you follow these simple practices, your life will change for the better... as Janet says, "CAUTION: Side effects may include: more laughter, more loving feelings, more happiness, more glee, more joy, and a lot of giggling ... Proceed at your own risk!"
— Steve Gaghagen

Janet is the most genuine, happy person on the inspirational scene, helping others bring joy to their life. *Get Stuck On Happy* effortlessly combines tools and examples designed for all to live their lives, as we should. HAPPY! Thank you Jan for your never-ending friendship and thank you for being you.   — Marg Pinard

I love it because it's the kind of book that you want to read and then refer back to at certain times in your life.   — Grace Brochu

Have you ever met someone and from the very first everything felt in sync? Like you were resuming a long, comfortable friendship? That is how it was for me meeting Janet. Although I feel very fortunate to call her my friend, I don't for a minute think I am in an elite group, as Janet makes everyone she touches feel that way. This lovely book embodies everything she is and gives us all the opportunity to live our best lives. Happiness is not based on grand gestures, rather simple, loving, heartfelt motions that when incorporated into your own life can change those around you exponentially. Be kind to yourself and read and practice each page...then share with all you know!
A heartfelt thank you, Janet.   — Terresa Burdick

Janet makes this journey a clear possibility for anyone willing to engage. Engage in your personal Happiness. As an educator and leader I appreciate when a complex challenge is simplified to enhance lives. Yours, mine, everyones. My school mantra was "How Could It Be Otherwise?" Janet, has the answer: We could all find Happiness! Join the journey to the life you deserve.
— P. Carvey, B.Sc., B.Ed., M.A.

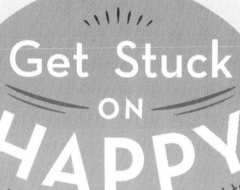

Get Stuck
ON
HAPPY

30 Ways to Change Your Thoughts
and Live a Happier Life

JANET LEGERE

Library and Archives Canada Cataloguing in Publication
Legere, Janet author Get Stuck on Happy / Janet Legere

Issued in print and electronic formats
ISBN 978-1-927897-12-6 (pbck)
ISBN 978-1-927897-13-3 (html)

www. getstuckonhappy.com

Printed in Canada

BE THAT
BOOKS™
PUBLISHING

Be Inspired.
Be Motivated.
Be Entertained.

*For my brother, Phil, and everyone who
is inspired to live a happier life!*

Table of Contents

Foreword

I grew up on the upper east side of Manhattan in the 1960's. The tall stately buildings on the wide West End Avenue were magnificent and hosted large apartments in big stone edifices. I have vivid memories of our living room as a child. A Baby Grand Steinway Piano stood at center stage. I've heard it said that the kitchen is the heart of the home, where families gather, cook, eat, share time and stories of their day with each other. I believe this to be true, however, a home with a Steinway has two hearts.

The Steinway is not just a musical instrument; the design, the craftsmanship, the presence, is a striking piece of art without one key being struck. When it is played, space and time are transformed into joy and dreams for all within hearing.

Being the 60's, my parents hosted very *hip* parties where well-dressed friends would gather, drink martini's, smoke cigarettes and speak esoterically. The chatter of the adults seemed loud and like a foreign language was being spoken that was totally incomprehensible to a child. The meaning behind the words was unimportant to me, I was waiting. Eventually, someone with magic in their fingers would approach the Steinway and run a hand lazily along its curved side, like a caress with promise, like stroking a sleeping cat. You could almost see the Steinway stretch and come to life.

Everyone waited for the moment. Magic was coming, the anticipation of the union of the player and the Steinway sucked all the noise away. The magic transformed the room, the quiet was focused, and directed at the Steinway and the musician with reverence. I loved the magic of the unison. I would awake the next morning still in its thrall.

During the afternoon the baby grand was taken over again as my older sister practiced and practiced, over, and over and over again. Pieces from Mozart, Beethoven, Bach, working on her own magic; magic not quite mature but with the Steinway, it was still magic. I admired her determination. I did not have the patience and envied her connection to the Steinway. Every day she played, our home was briefly transformed.

I remember *that* day. My sister was practicing and there came a **twang** from the Steinway as if injured. My whole body tensed, my mother stopped her needle point in the corner, my father stopped reading the paper, all eyes looking toward the Steinway. It sounded like no magic ever sounded. My sister started over and there it was again, **twang**. No matter how well-crafted the Steinway was, no matter how beautiful the design, or the brilliance of the composers, or the countless hours my sister poured into perfecting her art, nothing could stop the **twang**.

A few days later, the doorbell rang. My mother opened the door and there stood a thin man wearing a black suit with a wrinkled shirt, a thin black tie and a hat perched on top of his round head. His skin looked worn, with lines on his face that said, "I've seen sorrow and I've seen joy and I know the difference". Surely, Mom won't let him in our apartment. He was holding a black leather bag that looked like a doctor's house call bag, but no one was sick. My Mother greeted him like he was a prince, he nodded his greeting and walked right into our home and went right to our living room.

I was seven years old, he seemed ancient and he captured my imagination and interest. I could feel his intensity and focus; I knew he was on a mission. I watched as he shuffled through our home to stand before our Baby Grand Steinway piano. He held my entire attention and the Steinway held his. He put his bag down, murmured something that sounded like "Hello Sweetheart", ran his hand gently over the glossy, dustless top with one hand and walked all the way around the Steinway.

The old man pulled out a long metal tool, slightly resembling a salad fork, struck it and it vibrated. It seemed as though the air around it was moving and it emitted a ringing sound. He could read my fascination, and looked at me, motioned his head towards the space next to him on the seat and winked. I fearlessly jumped up next to him. I half-smiled up at him but my focus was on the tool. He struck it again and held it out for me to touch; it vibrated and produced a ringing sound. He lifted the lid on the Steinway and removed the felt strip over the top of the shiny black and white keys. I could hear him gently murmuring to the piano as he went, almost like seeking permission. "Such a beauty, ahhh here's the problem", then "this won't take too long", "must get you just right, you deserve the best". He placed his wrinkled hands on the keys, and began to play. It was magic, then it wasn't. "**Twang**".

He could see the worried look of concern on my face, leaned over and in a low whisper, as you'd use in church, said, "It's all about vibrations." He went on to explain how there are 88 keys, 230 strings, plus hammers, pins, and pedals which create the tones we hear by the strings vibration inside the Steinway. They must vibrate perfectly together each to their own frequency to get the sweetest sounds that brought the Steinway to life. He said, "We all get out of tune and just need our vibrations recalibrated now and then." He told me that each piano is different; how it is played, the weather, the way the wood stretches, the climate, everything will influence the sounds and the tones. He said you must pay attention to the unique qualities of each piano to get the most beautiful tones possible from it.

I stood on the bench and watched him strike the tuning fork and turn the pins attached to the strings, talking all the while to the piano as if it were a delicate lady. "Just a little more sweetheart, let's see how you sound now?" Time stood still as minutes turned into hours. I watched and listened, captivated by the process. He went back and forth pressing a key or two, then struck the tuning fork and turned one of the pins to adjust the tension on the string, bringing it to a perfect frequency. Back and forth, forth and back, he went adjusting, listening, and repeating, until he was satisfied with that string, then on to the next string. On and on it went, adjust, listen, repeat for hours. Finally, he sat down again and said, "She's ready". He placed his hands on the keys and started to play with stunning skill as though he was center stage at Carnegie Hall. My mother came in the room and sat and listened, a smile spread across her face as she sat in her chair. You could see the tension drain from her face, and I knew our world was back as it should be.

I have known Janet for a long time. Janet has always been a beautiful woman inside and out, and like so many of us, all her strings were not tuned to play the music she was capable of. She has worked hard, getting help from others, learning, getting herself tuned to the right vibrations to play the music of her life with brilliance. She enjoys sharing deep loving relationships with family, friends, and peers. She is endlessly giving and supportive. Her desire for each of us to live enriched lives bounces off the pages to vibrate right to our inner core.

I believe we each have beautiful music inside, we just need the right tuner to come into our lives and help us set our vibrations to the right frequencies. Pay close attention, Janet is ringing your doorbell, she has her black bag and she is about to take you on a journey to tune your life to the right vibrations. Once in tune, you still might hit that key that will go "twang". Then pick up the book and recalibrate your vibrations to fill your life with the brilliance of your music.

Carnegie Hall, here we come!

Devlyn Steele
March 2019

Introduction

Over the years I've called myself many names, not all nice. The label that was the initiator of this part of my journey was *survivor*. It was in the mid 90's that I challenged and took charge of the survivor character.

That character was created and molded by me as a little girl; a little girl who experienced sexual and physical abuse, from people who should have been trusted role models. There was very little trust and affirmation of my general goodness as a child. I learned survival skills that would see me through the tough times, but would leave hidden scars and memories.

As a child, I found ways to get attention. As a teenager, I strived to obtain love and acceptance, and as a young adult, I married my high school sweetheart providing me with a means of escape and possible happiness in a new start in life, away from my buried memories.

That new life created my three greatest treasures, my children. I always felt blessed and happy, even with my rocky foundation. As a family we moved frequently, which provided me with the opportunity to live and experience life as a family in Western Canada. Moving was fun and exciting; it always felt like a new start, a free do-over, and I liked that feeling.

Abuse doesn't leave the soul when you move, even if you move a lot. Abuse creates shame that leads to holes in your heart and soul that allows the joy of life to seep out, leaving you joyless, discontent and empty. By the time we settled in Calgary, a lot of joy had left my heart and soul, and I was spiraling downward and didn't know why.

I left my career as a successful corporate controller to help my husband establish a highly successful electronic and communication company. My children were entering their adolescent years and didn't need me in quite the same way as when they were younger. Teenager angst and pressures started increasing in our seemingly happy home and the holes in my heart and soul started leaking all the built up shame as joy evaporated out of my life. The happy facade of "the perfect, happy family" I had built evaporated along with the joy. The image of joy was still there, but for me the joy was gone. I felt empty and betrayed by my own hopes and dreams.

The residue that was left after the evaporation was a backpack of issues I had buried deep inside me; emotional scar tissue. I thought I had the life of my dreams, but it felt like ruin and unhappiness. When the facade of a perfect marriage started crumbling, the memories and negative self-talk erupted and spewed long buried memories into my mind that terrified me, and quite frankly puzzled me. I didn't want to go there, to remember, to relive and face the shame, but I went. I had a truckload of shame to deal with.

After a two year separation, my husband and I divorced and the real work on Janet's life began. I met my real self for the first time and I didn't like who I met. Trips to places I didn't want to visit, talks I didn't want to have and tears a child should have safely shed were some of the markers on my journey. I was a mess.

After twelve years of therapy, and the loving support of friends and family, the joy started returning and the holes in my heart and soul were mending, and when I talked to myself I found the image in the mirror smiling back with acceptance. There have been ups and downs, twists and turns, highs and lows, but now I'm stuck on happy, and I want *you* to be stuck on happy too. It has made me totally alive and whole again. Alive to sing (not that I should), to dance (not that I do), to play (this I do) and to be ridiculously happy in my life (every single day).

I was blessed to find the best support I could ever want near the middle of my journey. I was on the road to happiness when I found Mr. Right. Don is a source for my continued growth and optimism and has been my main cheerleader through the toughest parts of my journey and is my "partner in crime" through all the best parts. His support and nonjudgmental acceptance has made the fight for the right to have happiness meaningful and worthwhile. His empathy and support help me keep the shame in the *gone but not hidden* pile and the joy in the *here and now* pile. Now I'm in charge of my memories. My past is just that, memories of the journey that made me the good, happy, blessed person I am today.

I have surrounded myself with people who understand my journey, who support and accept the person I am today; full of life, joy and happiness, having had enough experience with darkness to have empathy and compassion for just about anyone.

In 2003, I met Devlyn Steele, a Life Coach from California who developed a system called Tools To Life[1]. He offered to mentor Don and me, and his mentorship has been a gift that keeps on giving. His coaching has transformed our lives. We discovered each other as autonomous individuals and as a devoted couple sharing a journey together; not competing or demanding, but supporting and listening with our hearts, not just our ears. We learned that our differences complimented our relationship and our similarities bonded us as a couple. As I began to discover a new way of thinking and responding, I found new sources of happiness to tap into. I was healing and deciding who and what I wanted to be, and I chose to be Happy! Happy for me, not because of events around me, but because I like Happy! I like the feeling of Happy; the joyful heart, the face in the mirror that says it's going to be a beautiful day, my choice, and yes, my control. I found that my happiness was contagious and it spread to others that touched my life, my family, my friends, my associates; my happiness was contagious.

In 2012, it was suggested by one of my webinar attendees, that I produce a daily motivational call. At first, a little voice in my head said "you have NO time for another webinar" (I was already presenting 5-6 times a week), "you aren't good enough to inspire others". As self doubt took over, I felt my happiness decrease as negativity entered my heart and began to influence my life. I talked to Don, my rock. He was so supportive and positive; how could I doubt myself? Of course I should take the risk and give it my best effort. I packed up my self-doubt and took the risk of offering up my heart and soul to others as a gift of gratitude for the journey and resultant life I had. Every weekday morning, I started my day with a brief webinar addressing how to find happiness and joy in everyday life. Now, I am a gifted, happy talker; I can do it all day, all night, all week (ask anyone that knows me). My Happy came back bigger and brighter than ever when I began *The Morning Motivator*[2]. For five years, every Monday to Friday a few dedicated individuals attended the live calls and worked with and through me to increase their happiness quotient and get motivated to find success.

As a group, we experienced many breakthroughs and "aha" moments in the quest of happiness. The result of one of those "aha" moments is the book you now hold. I often contemplated writing my story, but I didn't want to focus on the abuse. One day as I was meditating, it all came together for me; write a practical book about happiness, a simple, portable plan in a book.

I hope that this book will inspire and guide you to find a little bit of happiness everywhere you go and in everything you do. As you practice and manifest the concepts and exercises, you will discover that you have a more positive outlook, better relationships, and are more productive with your time, because you are *Happier*. Dr. Lee Jampolsky, author of *Smile For No Good Reason* reminds us, you always have a choice to be "happy inside, no matter what is going on outside"[3].

We don't always like or choose the events that show up in our lives, but our attitude about what shows up is always a choice. I am honoured to be part of your journey.

I hope that as you read you will discover your own happiness. Continue to apply the tips and techniques from *Get Stuck On Happy* and your journey will be all the better for it!

Daily Vibrational Cards

Every being on this planet is nothing more than energy. Each person's energy vibrates at different frequencies. High vibrations, or frequencies, correspond with feelings of positive energy like joy and happiness. Low vibrations, or frequencies, are the results of feelings of negative energy, like sadness or anger. The more we understand the vibrational nature, the more we understand how our feelings are related to it. It is important to practice choosing good vibrations daily; remember, the vibrations you send out are the vibrations you get back.

Each day, as you continue your activities, you will be guided to create a *Vibration Card* to remind you to increase your awareness and choose positivity. You can create your own, or use the suggestions in the book. It's fun to get a little creative and decorate your cards with stickers or artwork. You can also leave them plain.

I repurpose old business cards and write a word or message on the back. If you like, you can pick up blank business card sheets at your local stationery store and use those. Any handy paper will do. You can even use your phone or a screen saver banner. A friend uses recipe cards that she cuts in half for convenience sake. Don uses post-it notes.

The key to this exercise is to *read and reflect on the cards regularly and let the vibration refresh you.*

With each new card you create, you will be adding to your own personal deck of *Happiness*. This deck can be as large or small as you like.

Review a few cards from your deck of *Happiness* each day and be refreshed and renewed by the positive words. For instance, if you have written *More Love* on the card, reflect on the feeling of having more love in your life. Focus on how amazing it feels, bask in it, and breathe in the energy. Prepare yourself to accept *more*.

Here are a few of my personal Vibrational Cards. More Love, More Abundance, More Joy. Each of these cards builds and reinforces my happy vibrations. I continue to reflect on these cards. They have become my present reality; they help me to create the *Happiness* I desire and deserve.

30 Ways to Change Your Thoughts

The following pages will guide you through thirty activities that will assist you in creating change in your current patterns of thinking and responding. You are in charge of your thoughts.

The most important aspect of these activities is to recognize when your thoughts drift from the positive to the negative. When this happens, immediate change needs to occur in your thinking process to change your energy. The more you practice these activities, the more tools you will create to combat negative thoughts and energies that enter your day.

Sadness, jealousy, anger, self-doubt, and fear are examples of negative thoughts that can typically pass through your day. Any thought that drains your energy is a negative thought, and it's up to you to stop at that moment and decide to change what you are thinking about, change the situation, or change your response to the situation.

The sooner you recognize that your energy has decreased, the sooner you can take action to change your thoughts and move you closer to happier feelings. Using your vibration cards and the skills you will learn will guide you to *think yourself happy*. With continued practice, you can think yourself happy almost instantly!

CAUTION: Side effects may include more laughter, more loving feelings, more happiness, more glee, more joy, and a lot of energy, Proceed at your own risk!

⟶ 1 ⟵
Decide to Have A Great Day

In 2002 I met Devlyn Steele, who became a very special friend. It was a connection that altered the way Don and I approach our days. Devlyn is a life coach, author, and the CEO of *Tools To Life*. We chatted about his program and he offered to coach Don and me. Don joined the conversation and we agreed to devote eleven weeks to his program. And so our journey began.

During our journey, we were introduced to many tools. These tools soon became habits; we changed our thought processes, which changed our feelings and responses to all situations.

One of the first exercises we learned in the Tools to Life Program, and one we continue to practice faithfully to this day, is so simple, you will be happy to practice it! I share it because it has an immediate effect on how you feel and how you approach your day.

Tool #1 from Tools To Life:

First thing in the morning when you wake up, don't lay around in bed contemplating the snooze button. Get up, plant your feet solidly on the floor, stand up and clap your hands together and, with a smile, say out loud: "**I'm having a GREAT Day!**" Go through your morning routine and as you go by a mirror, look yourself in the eye, smile, and say "**I'm having a GREAT Day!**" Do it with enthusiasm and remember to smile; you just empowered your day to become a GREAT one!

Every morning when you get up, decide to have a great day. Add this little ritual to your regular routine and you will be amazed at how quickly your days are enhanced when you declare to yourself, with personal intention, that you are "**having a GREAT Day!**" Repeat this anytime during the day when you find your energy draining or unwanted negativity slipping in. You CAN have a GREAT day everyday!

"Have a GREAT Day!"

*Create the Vibration Card now
and let more energy flow through you.*

MORE Energy

∾ 2 ∾
Place Happy Things Around You

During our Morning Motivator webinars ideas fly through cyberspace, as we work together to get our day going in a positive, productive direction. I am inspired by the people I meet and the friends I have made. The Morning Motivator not only inspires me, it also makes me happy to be part of people's morning routines.

Being happy is a choice, a decision to be made. There are times when we may need a little prompting to see the choice and adjust our responses. This exercise can help you maintain or recover your focus and can be applied anywhere.

Start with your home. Walk into each room and look around. Is there something in that room that makes you happy? Can you see something that brings back a happy memory? If the answer is no, put something in that room that brings you joy; maybe a memento of a trip, a picture of a loved one, a favourite hobby object or something that brings you positive energy. If you can't find something that makes you happy, pop up a sticky note that says: *Smile,* or *Be Happy,* as a little reminder to smile and be happy. Extend this practice to all the places you regularly spend time; your office, your wallet, your car, your brief-case, your computer screen.

Your space is important and should be a reflection of you and where your focus is. Create spaces that encourage happy. This will help you maintain your focus and give you a little positive boost of happy during your day, no matter where you are.

My home office is where I spend the majority of my time. It is absolutely loaded with things that make me smile. Recently, Don came into my office and a huge smile spread across his face as he scanned all the pictures drawn by our grandchildren, the plants, cards from friends and teddy bear figures. Everywhere I look in my office, I see something that makes me smile or that reminds me of the love that surrounds me. Every room in our home is the same. There is a piece of happiness somewhere in every room that brings a smile to my face and joy to my heart when my eyes scan past it. Make sure you add some *happy* to your spaces!

Create your Vibration Card now
and let feelings of joy fill your heart.

More
JOY!

～ 3 ～
Breathe

Breathing is essential for life. It connects us directly to our environment and is associated with calming emotions and soothing frazzled nerves and tense muscles. It is essential that we capitalize on breathing to bring us back to a more peaceful state of being. Incorporating a breathing exercise into your regular routine will support and nurture your ability to respond and increase your happiness quotient.

Perform this exercise several times a day or more if you are feeling anxious, have low energy or feel emotionally drained. Take a deep breath in, right down to your belly and hold it, while thinking about something that brings you joy. SMILE, then exhale fully, using your tummy muscles to completely push the used air out of your lungs. Repeat this exercise two or three times and you will notice an improvement in how you feel.

When you inhale, focus on breathing in more joy and let it settle throughout your body; every muscle, every nerve, every cell.

When you exhale, visualize relaxation and the shedding of everything that does not serve your current needs. Let it flow away with the expended air and remember to smile.

Once you create a deck of vibration cards, you can draw out five or so and on your inhale, say the words on your vibration card (to yourself) "more love, more harmony, more creativity, more connection" and on the exhale say them a second time. "I give love, harmony, creativity, connection". Changing your cards around is a great review and helps to reestablish your focus and priorities.

After you perform the exercise three to five times, say a positive affirmation to enhance positive self talk, such as "I feel calm and peaceful", "I am loved and valued just as I am", or "I can make this a great day!" This exercise can be done anywhere, anytime, and as often as you like.

*Create your Vibration Card now
and enjoy the peaceful balance of connecting deeply
with your surroundings and your body as you breathe.*

MORE
Balance!

~ 4 ~
Words of Gratitude

Start a gratitude journal and commit to writing in it every day for thirty days. Read at least one entry, other than the current day, each day. Gratefulness is a way to connect your mind and heart with those around you. There are so many things to be grateful for and recognizing them will bring you happiness. At first, you may simply make a list. Later on, try to expand your list and define how, and why, each thing is involved in your gratitude and happiness. Being grateful for the little things in your life shifts your energy and will make you feel more connected and whole.

Day 1 — at the beginning of your day, write down three things you are grateful for. Regardless of where you are in life, there are always many things to be grateful for. You can even change your negatives into positives.

> **Negative:** "I couldn't do my exercises today because I had too much laundry to do."
> **Positive:** "I am so grateful that I have all these clothes!"
> **Negative:** "I have all these dishes to wash."
> **Positive:** "I am so grateful for the lovely dinner we just enjoyed."

At the end of your day, write down three more things that you are grateful for. Number one might be that you made it through the day! Perhaps you found a parking spot in a packed parking lot, or maybe someone kindly offered assistance when you had a challenge. Our days are filled with the opportunity to demonstrate gratitude; you won't have to look too far. I'm always grateful when another driver knows the difference between a yield and merge sign; it warms my heart every time!

Some people write their gratitude on the back of their Vibration Cards as a handy way to be reminded of gratitude throughout the day.

Day 2 onward — Spend time each morning and evening writing down at least three things you are grateful for. As your gratitude journal fills, spend time each day reviewing at least three days of past entries. Remind yourself of the gratefulness and how connected you are to your surroundings.

I am grateful you have made it this far and I know that if you write in your gratitude journal every day, your life will change and it will positively impact the lives around you. Please spread the happiness around; if your gratitude is connected to someone, tell them. It will increase their happiness too!

Make your Vibration Card now and let the joy
of Gratitude move in your heart.

MORE
Gratitude!

～ 5 ～
Think on Purpose

How many times are you operating on "autopilot" during the day? We all do it more than we even realize; responding and reacting to situations and events without any real thought at all. It's human nature; our brains know what to do in many circumstances. I am grateful for that reflex when the car in front of me slams on their brakes, but not so thankful when I zone out during a meeting. We get easily bored and allow our brains to control us; sometimes good, sometimes not so good. We need to be in control and observant, to live our lives with purpose.

Thinking on purpose means choosing your thoughts and learning to stay present in your day, all day long. When you zone out, you lose valuable time and are less efficient. How you respond to situations is often far more important than the situation itself. You need clear input from your surroundings to make choices. Choosing to control your attention and think on purpose will help you through difficult and challenging situations. Enhanced connectedness to your environment and the people around you will stimulate creativity and team building as you build skills by thinking on purpose.

If, as Earl Nightingale says, "Everyone of us is the sum total of all our thoughts" it makes sense to choose happy, joyful, positive thoughts, and lots of them! Choose to stay focused, choose to think about the person you are with, choose to be present in every moment.

Thinking negative thoughts will drain away your energy and the energy of those around you, slowing productivity and diminishing joy and happiness. Negativity can easily become a bad habit and will drain away the desire and focus to be happy. When you find yourself entering the spiral of negativity, take charge, practice breathing, check out your vibration cards, and make a conscious shift to think on purpose. You are in charge of you, and you are the only one that can change you, so be purposeful and joyful in your thinking processes if you want to be joyful and happy, in your life. Joyful thoughts make you joyful and happy, and that happiness is contagious; you will create more positive energy for yourself and for those around you.

Choose thoughts that support how you want to feel. When you are feeling anxious about something such as your job, relationships or finances, ask yourself, "What one positive action could I take to lessen the anxiety?" Focus on that one thing. Be in charge of you and create change; create positive change, even if it seems like just small steps. Every thought you change from negative to positive gives you a new door to open and a new path to go down. You are in charge of you and your thoughts, so take positive control! Choose to walk a happy path!

The past is gone, the future is not here yet; stay in the moment.

Make your Vibration Card now, at this very moment!

MORE
Purpose!

❦ 6 ❧
Meditate

Meditation is a practice that looks simple on the outside but takes focus, effort, and desire. It produces immediate benefits for the body, mind, and spirit and promotes better health. Meditation is even used by children to change, or modify, unwanted behavior. Baltimore, Maryland's Robert W. Coleman Elementary School[4] has been utilizing meditation since 2016. The school created a *Mindful Moment Room*, where students who act in a manner that disrupts learning or display socially unacceptable behavior are sent, or can request to go to focus and breathe in a calm, quiet environment. The outcome is nothing short of amazing. At Coleman Elementary, children who use the *Mindful Moments Room* become more internally focused, kind and happy.

Meditation is different for everyone and you will find your own personal rhythm. The goal is to reach the stillness that promotes peace and a sense of wellbeing. Meditation does not need to be long or arduous. It may, however, be a challenge to calm your mind; to breathe and to be mindful simultaneously. Ten to twenty minutes of guided or silent meditation per day is a great way to begin.

Find a place where you won't be interrupted for your time allocation. Sit in a comfortable position, but not so comfortable that you sleep. This is not a power nap, this is *focused attention* on you. Do not put your head down on your desk.

The key to meditation is breathing. In technique #3 BREATHE, you started a regime of focused breathing and hopefully are continuing that practice. Meditation will use a similar technique. Breathe in good positive energy and breathe out all the stress and worries, clearing the mind of external influences as the ten or so minutes pass. As your breathing calms and the feelings of angst of the day dissipate, feel your body systems relax; your heart, your lungs, the muscles in your neck and shoulders, arms and legs. Relax each muscle group as you identify it. As you practice meditation, you will be more in control of each body group and will be able to relax each group separately, and on demand. Be mindful that your breathing remains calm and regular throughout the exercise.

We tend to focus our attention everywhere but where we are. We worry about the future and fret about the past. We live only in a brief moment caught between the two. The here and now is where you need to focus your attention on this exercise. Meditation is a great tool for anchoring yourself in the present, even if for only a few minutes. Give yourself the gift of ten minutes. Nothing in your world will collapse if you are absent for ten minutes. Give yourself permission to make your well being a priority. This is not self-indulgence; this is life. And yours is valuable.

With regular meditation practice, you will create a safe haven inside yourself; a calmer heart, lower blood pressure, a clearer mind, and a more relaxed body. All of these attributes will make you better at decision making, more confident, a stronger leader, and a more positive person as you interact with those around you.

Your meditation is a warm,
calming solution for the overburdened mind.

Make your Vibration Card now and take a few minutes
to begin your meditation practice.

MORE
Meditation!

~ 7 ~
Find a Fun Distraction

I remember one day I was very upset about something. I couldn't tell you what it was now, but I can remember the feeling of anxiety. My emotions were unruly and my happy buttons were definitely not on. I came down to the kitchen and said, "Don, I need you to make me feel better". Don, in his infinite wisdom replied, "I can't make you feel better, only you can do that". I took a deep breath and rather than beat him over the head, I said, " I know you can't, but I need a distraction. Can you distract me, I'm stuck." Well, distraction is evidently one of Don's gifts! Within minutes I was smiling and laughing, and my positive energy was quickly on the rise.

Had Don not been there, I could have chosen to go for a walk or even call a friend for a little positive distraction. When negative thoughts and emotions have you stuck in a rut, you have to make a shift, and realize you are in control. Laugh at yourself, call a friend, look at your happy things, laugh out loud at an old memory. Decide to go to a happy place.

More Fun is where life is best
and more fun always leads to Happiness.

Make your Vibration Card now and have a good laugh.
Let the laugh wash through you, then laugh some more!

MORE
Fun!

∽ 8 ∼
Determine your Intention

An exercise in *Ask and It is Given*[5] is to give intention to your day. I want to break it down into segments. Before you start any activity, visualize how that activity will ideally go and the desired outcome of the activity. See the possibilities. The intention is more than a goal. It is a *visualization* of an outcome. Take some time to visualize the activity.

For example, you need groceries, and have prepared a list. Visualize your drive to the store. It is smooth sailing; each light that you come upon turns immediately green. You drive to the front of the lot and there is a nice big wide parking spot open. See your trip down the aisles; everything you want is in stock, you are able the select the best, freshest produce to maintain your healthy lifestyle. When you have your groceries and are ready to check out, voila, no line! Your groceries scan without any issues, they are securely packed and loaded in your car. When you get home, all green lights, of course, you unpack your groceries and can see all the meals you will be able to create with the bounty. When finished, add a little gratitude to the equation; thank-you for the farmers, the truck drivers, the clerks, for making your life so good.

Here is an intentional affirmation to remind you to look for the happiness everywhere you go, and in everything you do today and every day.

*Today, no matter where I am going, no matter
what I am doing, no matter who I am doing it with,
I will make it my dominant intention to look for things that
feel good. When I feel good, I am vibrating with my Higher Power.*

Create your Vibration Card now.

MORE
Good
Intentions!

~ 9 ~
Let It Go

Letting go can be difficult and challenging at the best of times, and yet it is one habit that is essential to cultivate happiness. When you hold on to negative energy, it depletes your ability to maintain and grow positive energy. It takes a tremendous amount of your positive energy to hold on to useless negative energy. Often, your negative energy has become such a familiar part of your life, you don't realize you are carrying it around; it just slowly depletes your positive energy and puts you in a deficit.

You have had many years getting used to ignoring and carrying your negative energy around. It is important to develop awareness of your personal energy, when it comes and when it goes. Become aware of practices that keep you on the positive side of energy usage. Awareness of the useless negative energy you sustain will help you release it before you get used to having it around. It serves no purpose other than draining your positive energy.

When letting go of the negative, you will be making room for more positive energy. Releasing the negative energy will help you create balance in your life and ultimately make room for more joy and happiness.

One of my favorite ways to let go is listening to a guided meditation by Lori Granger[6], LMFT, called *Let Go* (You can search for Lori Granger on YouTube). This fifteen-minute meditation is very simple to follow. Just sit in your chair, relax and follow Lori's guidance. You will be amazed at how quickly fifteen minutes can go by and how great you will feel at the end of the meditation. Another way to help rid yourself of negative energy is to allow yourself 5 minutes to write out the angst of the negativity, then rip it up into small pieces and throw it away, or flush it down a toilet. Enjoy the release of ridding yourself of that worry.

Practice letting go and create this Vibration Card right now!

MORE
Release!

⁓ 10 ⁓
Practice Yoga

Yoga is a simple practice that can help you start or end your day by aligning your mind, body, and soul. You will feel calm, relaxed and balanced when finished and you will carry a sense of calmness and wellness into your day, and night.

Practicing yoga does not need to be difficult or lengthy; five to ten minutes of yoga every day can bring about a dramatic change in your life. Yoga is not a religion, nor does it require that you get fully into postures (asanas) to reap benefits. Don't worry about flexibility. The central idea is calm breathing through balanced movement and being totally present in your body. If you are not flexible, that may improve with practice; the only prerequisite is willingness and desire.

There are many ways to practice yoga. I started by going on YouTube and searching for *beginners yoga*. Doing the Sun Salutation with Rodney Yee is a perfect fit for Don and Me. I often do a second *yoga for beginners* to relieve muscle stress during the day. Many people buy a DVD with an entire yoga series available to them at the click of the remote. Yoga studios are located in easy driving distance to practically everywhere. Yoga studios offer a range of classes, from hot yoga to classes for only men, only women, mixed, or seniors. There is one nearby for you to try it out.

Life is divine when we sit with wellness. In wellness, we feel strong, confident and whole. Make your wellness card now, and let the warmth of wellness shower over you all through your day.

Create your Vibration Card now.

MORE
Wellness!

~ 11 ~
Hug Someone

4 Hugs a Day, that's the minimum. 4 Hugs a Day, NOT the maximum...

My granddaughters used to sing this little song by Charlotte Diamond[7] to me each year at the Mother's Day tea at their preschool and kindergarten. This little song touched my heart because it speaks the truth; hugs heal.

We are social beings, we crave social interaction and connection. Take the time to give a good hug to someone today, and in return, you will get one back!

When you give a hug, hold the person you are hugging for a few seconds, don't let go right away, and as you give your hug, let your positive energy flow through your arms into them. Relax your body into the hug. A good three-second hug is worth enough positive energy to make it through the toughest day.

4 Hugs a Day, that's the minimum. 4 Hugs a Day, NOT the maximum . . . give and receive as many hugs as you can!

We all need more hugs in our lives.
Hugs comfort us and remind us that we are not alone.

Make your Vibration Card now
then sit in the warmth of having a hug.

MORE
Hugs!

～ 12 ～
Act Like a Kid

When we were children we were told not to act like a baby. When we were teenagers, we are told not to act like a child. As an adult, we are told not to act like a baby, child, or be immature; take your pick. In truth, we need to act 'young'; to have the pure heart and exuberance of a child. As adults, we take ourselves so seriously we forget about the simple joys and pleasures in life. Watch a child at play, and you will see joy and happiness in the smallest of events.

I love being able to spend time with our grandchildren. Watching them play is enlightening and always brings me joy. Children have no fear, they are full of imagination, and ready to try anything. They love unconditionally, get mad and forgive completely. Let's not abandon these choice characteristics! Let's resolve instead to recover these attributes!

My grandson loves to fall down, for no reason at all. If he is playing catch or anything sport-like and misses the ball, he just falls down and giggles and laughs. One afternoon, his mom, pointedly asked me "Why does he do that?" I thought for a minute. Attention seeking? Pride? Distraction? In the end I replied with "*Because it's fun*". Children don't have reasons for everything; if it makes them laugh, or others laugh, they are all in. They embrace fun and they fall into it and roll around in it. If there isn't any fun around, they create it.

Embrace your inner child and have fun today! Act like a big kid in something you do; enjoy it for the pure unadulterated fun of it, laugh at it, laugh at yourself. When you take yourself too seriously for too long, you forget about how spontaneous joy and fun can be, and how powerful it is as a positive energy source. Be brave! Embrace your inner child and come out to play!

Find something fun to play today and every day.

Make your Vibration Card now and remember that fun and joy and happiness are all connected. Have fun being playful!

MORE Play!

~ 13 ~
Call a Friend

Most of us have someone we can call. Friends can be a great diversion when we are feeling negative, their voice can work as a tool to give us the positive energy we are lacking. Reaching out to friend or family connects us and enriches our lives.

If you are feeling like you have no one to call or connect with, that is your negative energy taking over. Take charge and decide that the happy you is going to connect with friends and family even if it has been a long time. Break the time barrier and re-establish the connection.

There are so many ways to connect with people; phone, text, Skype and the best yet, in person. Reaching out is the key. We need to ask for the connection, as it will not happen if you sit back and wait. Take the initiative to share your energy through a friendship connection.

Remember that there are times when your friends or family will reach out to you in need of positive energy. They may not even realize that is what they are seeking. When you give them that boost of energy, that connection, your energy will not be diminished. Your positive energy will actually multiply. Remember not to take on anyone else's negative energy as your own. Let them choose to let it go and know that it is not for you to pick up and carry as your own. Empathy is good, yet ownership of someone else's negativity is not necessary nor healthy.

Remember, do not focus only on complaining about your situation. Do not burden someone with your negative energy. Talking through a concern is a great way to share with friends and family, but be mindful not to get stuck in the negative. Remember why you are connecting;

exchange positivity. Letting someone know they are valued and cared for will immediately cause their energy to rise and that positive energy will boomerang to you immediately. You just have to accept the positive energy when it comes your way!

Friends are like hugs — you can never have too many!

Make your Vibration Card now and savor the feeling of having more, wonderful, caring friends. You are not alone.

MORE Friends!

∾ 14 ∾
What Can I Do To Make This Different

If you find yourself in a situation that is not pleasant, the first thing to do is take a self-inventory. Acquaint yourself with your feelings and your actions. Did you contribute to some of the unpleasantness? If you were instrumental, or contributed, to the creation of negative energy, go back to your cards and review each one, seeking to restore your positive energy. Unravel the actions as quickly as possible so the least number of people are harmed by that negative energy.

If you continue to engage in the negative feelings of sadness, anger, anxiety, or frustration, you will persist in losing more and more positive energy, creating a downward spiral. Once you have an awareness of your feelings, stop and take a deep breath, all the way down to your belly and slowly breathe out. Practice your breathing exercises from the technique #3 BREATHE, until you feel your calm return. Ask yourself if there is anything you can do to make the situation different in a more positive way. Trust your positive self to make the situation different. What are the steps you can personally initiate to affect change? Be very honest with yourself. If you contributed negatively, fix it.

In some situations, you may not have very much control or power to initiate change. In such cases, make sure you come to full awareness of the circumstances that concern you and change your response toward the situation. This will be a challenge at first, as we are conditioned to be reactive rather than responsible. We are conditioned to think "If I didn't do it, it's not my problem to fix it". You might not be able to fix the situation, but you certainly don't have to wallow negatively in a bad situation. As you become more intune with your feelings, you will be able to shift your reactions *before* the negativity overcomes your positive energy. You will also be more mindful of your contributions to group energy dynamics.

In any situation, remember, that you can only change you. No matter what your position, you *cannot change someone else*. You may be able to dictate what someone does, but not how they feel. Your reactions define your experiences and energy levels. Hate your job or boss? If you cannot change your job or your boss, you have to change your *thinking*. Find positive aspects of your job or boss that *are* positive. Focus on the awesome things and do not dwell on the negative aspects.

Awareness helps you maintain honesty and integrity,
and helps you determine your options and responses. Wake up
awareness and let it flow through every breath you take.

Create your Vibration Card now.

MORE
Awareness!

∽ 15 ∽
Check You Attitude

How you respond to situations relates to your attitude. You are in control of your attitude. Check your attitude; make sure you are not dragging negative energy into everything you do with your interpretation and outward responses to events. What are your feelings as you work through a situation? Is your mental state making your interactions positive or negative? What are you thinking about? Where are your thoughts focused? Be honest with how you are feeling; not judgemental, but honest. Try to engage with some mental positivity before you begin publically troubleshooting an issue.

You can find something positive in everything you do. Remember to use technique #4 GRATITUDE. Using this card in conjunction with your attitude will bring your positive attitude into focus. Acknowledge your feelings, figure them out and deal with them. Don't dwell and wallow on negative feelings, or your energy will degrade quickly. Find parts of your situation that are positive, check your attitude and feel the difference. Be grateful you have found some positive aspects of your current situation. This attitude change will make you emotionally strong and resilient.

Being honest with yourself is a great act of self-love and respect. When you are honest with yourself, you demonstrate kindness and acceptance to yourself. If you find you are feeling, mad, frustrated, lost, angry, dissatisfied, judgemental; don't continue on that path of destruction. You are only hurting yourself and removing the positive energy from your day. Acknowledge what you are feeling and decide to make a shift by connecting to something that feels better, more positive, and more supportive.

Notice that the situation did not change. You changed your attitude. You *are* in control of your feelings and attitude as well as how they are expressed. When you shift your focus from the negative to the positive, your attitude will shift too. You will be helping yourself and those around you.

If you must be in close proximity to someone who exudes negativity, try to change your outlook to help them focus. Demonstrate so much positivity that it flows over into their personal space. Don't allow anyone's negativity to dictate your own energy.

To quote Monty Python:
"Always look on the Bright Side of Life".

There is a bright side to every situation.
Be kind and loving to yourself, focus there.

Create your Vibration Card now.

MORE
Brightness!

~ 16 ~
Tell Someone They Matter

Let people know they matter to you. Feeling valued is important for personal growth and leads to happiness. Everyone you come in contact with matters and should be valued. Let them know. You might be the only person who gives them positive energy in their day.

Here are some simple statements that will do the job nicely:

- ♥ Great job today — Thank you!
- ♥ Thank you so much. Have a great day!
- ♥ You are doing a great job and I appreciate it so much!
- ♥ Your smile really brings this place to life!

Your kind words matter. Find something positive to say to everyone that you interact with; friends, family, co-workers, acquaintances and total strangers. They matter and should feel like a valued part of your environment. Consider every interaction you have as environmental maintenance.

When you tell others they matter, you will increase your value and matter more to them. You will get positive energy back and every day will be better than the last.

It feels great to be appreciated.
It validates our effort and our very existence.

Make your Vibration Card now and sit with appreciation.
It feels wonderful to receive it, and it's a joy to express it.

MORE
Appreciation!

✎ 17 ✎
Buy Flowers

Everyone can use a little more kindness and thoughtfulness. Bringing good things into your life and the lives of others is simple. One easy way to add a little goodness to your day is to buy flowers. Flowers add life, color, and joy to any space. Most people love flowers and they lift the positive energy level in any room.

Flowers represent new life, happiness, springtime, and joy. When you bring, or display, flowers you display these feelings and share them with others. Even the single stem of a flower will add joy to any space.

Flowers are a simple way to add goodness to your life. Treat yourself and others with the gift of beauty, life and viality. Add flowers to your home, your office and your friends lives. Take time to stop and enjoy flowers anytime you see them. Admire their beauty, take time to inhale their beautiful scent and gently feel their soft and glorious petals. Stop, and smell the flowers . . . but first, get some!

Create your Vibration Card now,
and let more simple goodness bloom in your heart!

MORE
Flowers!

~ 18 ~
Express a Little Love

Take an intimacy break. If you have a partner, find time to cuddle, snuggle or caress. Connect in an intimate way. Intimacy elevates your serotonin levels and leads to a sense of well being and general happiness. Take time every day to demonstrate to your partner that you love them and that being with them brings you joy and fulfillment.

As you move through your day stop and make physical contact. A hand on the shoulder, a soft kiss on the cheek, or just saying "I love you". Use your imagination and make sure your partner knows they are a source of joy and happiness to you.

No partner? Tell a friend, aunt, father, sister or child how much you love and appreciate them. Write yourself a note of appreciation in your gratitude journal. Volunteer at a shelter and show the world the kindness and love inside of you. My friend volunteers in a seniors' home and visits regularly with seniors that have no visitors. She showers them with love and affection because she has it and they need it. In return, she is showered in love and appreciation.

Love is the highest vibration enhancer.

Make your Vibration Card now and think about those you love and love you. Let that love flow from your mind to your heart, wrap your arms around that feeling.

~ 19 ~
Check in

Take a few minutes each day to check in with your: mind, body, and spirit. Ask yourself, "How am I feeling emotionally?", "How does my body feel?", "Am I grounded in my day?", "What extraneous thoughts are clouding my judgment?", "Am I on a positive path or have I been sidetracked?"

While you're taking inventory of you, don't be distracted by stimuli from your immediate environment. Take a moment to breathe in and out a few times, slowly, and remember to smile. Complete your inventory and decide whether or not you need to shift gears.

Once you have completed your self-awareness inventory, determine what you need to do differently. You've got this. Adjust your day as needed. All is well.

Self-awareness is the ability to evaluate yourself at any time.
Spend time with yourself, only you can change you and
only you can verify that all your systems are in alignment.
Take the time to ensure your needs are being met.

Create your Vibration Card now.

MORE
Self-Awareness!

~ 20 ~
Accept and Move On

Every experience offers you one of two things; a valuable lesson, or a tremendous blessing. In every situation, pause and think:

- ♥ "What is the lesson in this for me?"
- ♥ "Is there a blessing for me?"
- ♥ "How does this affect the people around me?"

When you have choices to make, your whole body undergoes change. Ensure that you are thinking "lesson or blessing", not a quick and easy fix. It's important to be honest with yourself and review the big picture in any situation, not just your tiny part in it. Once you decide on "lesson or blessing", it's time to accept it and move on.

Don't wallow in negative situations for long. Find something positive about the situation, **accept and move on**. Allow yourself to move forward in freedom, without negative thoughts or emotions nagging you for days (or weeks or months!). If what is happening is completely beyond your control, shift your attention from the negative aspects and focus on the positive.

Remember, this process isn't just about you, this is about what's best for the whole system. Back-up, push the pause button and check how this experience is affecting your day, and possibly your life. Know that you are not alone; you are part of a huge system.

Focus on the positive, be grateful for the lesson, enjoy the blessings and continue your journey in the directions of Happiness.

Freedom is a choice. It is filled with light and joy.
Accept what you cannot change, learn the lesson,
accept the blessings. Let the feeling of freedom bloom for you.

Create your Vibration Card now.

MORE
Freedom!

～ 21 ～
Get Outside

Nature is a great way to realign yourself. The scents and colors of nature are essential to your senses and well being. Nature is everywhere; go to a park, stroll beside a river or stream, take a drive. A tree-lined street in your neighbourhood will do! Get outside and breathe the air of your environment and immerse yourelf in nature.

Stop and feel the energy of the universe you are surrounded by. Its power and influence is everywhere you go. Allow yourself to harmonize with nature. Let it into your day. Listen for it and hear the music of birds singing all around you. Let the colours fill your gaze; the vibrant pink, yellow, and purple of the flowers, the varying shades of green at every turn. Allow the scent of the cool forest to fill you with calm. It's all available for you, all the time, free of charge!

Nature will nurture your positive energy, but you must take the opportunity to see it first, then interact with it and respect it. Observe the many aspects of nature, the animals, the insects, the plants, wind, the changing seasons. Open your senses and let nature be part of your day, everyday!

The variety of nature is a simple way to get your happy on!

Create your Vibration Card now.

MORE Nature!

22
Say Yes

I learned this strategy from E Squared (E²) by Pam Grout[8]. Make today a YES day. This means that you are going to answer in the affirmative to everything! The key to this exercise is to ensure you are in the right frame of mind. The wrong frame of mind could result in negative experiences, and that is not where you want to go! The goal is to create joy, excitement and adventure.

The correct mindset is one that embraces a sense of joyful expectation so make this your starting point. Jump into your day expecting that every choice you make will be a perfect choice and that every moment of your day will be part of a joyful adventure. Yes! I will go for a walk in the park. Yes! I will take a little risk that frightens me. Yes! I will treat myself to a banana split.

Saying Yes! with joyful expectation paves the way for exciting and fulfilling experiences and a whole lot of happy! Every day has the potential to be a YES! day and may lead to a more interesting future, so please say Yes!

You did not sign up for a lifetime of ordinary.

Make your adventure Vibration Card and imagine all the little ways you can infuse adventure into each day. You are extraordinary!

MORE Adventure!

~ 23 ~
Talk To Your Future Self

Have you ever given thought to your future self? That person who is living the life you currently dream of? The you that you are becoming. It's a great experience to consult the 'future you' from time to time, to verify that the life you are living supports the dreams you are dreaming. 'Future you' will have unique ideas and insights. After all, they are living the life you dream of. A great question to ask is: "What would my future self do?"

Think about that question, meditate on it, picture 'future you' in action! How would your future self respond to a given situation?

- ♥ What actions would 'future you' take to improve the situation?
- ♥ What actions would 'future you' not take?
- ♥ Where would 'future you' go for help?
- ♥ Who would 'future you' talk to?
- ♥ How would 'future you' feel about the situation?

Think of the implications of looking into your future. Let your imagination run wild with ideas and you will be amazed. Remember 'future you' is you, just with more experience, more confidence and more journey to draw from.

Sitting with confidence is grounding and affirming.
It feels amazing when you really know and connect
with your ability to move in the direction of your dreams.
Be confident that you will find a way. Own your destiny!

Create your Vibration Card now.

MORE Confidence!

~ 24 ~
Change The Scenery

When the situation you are in is not supporting you, it may be time for a change of scenery. A scenery change can allow your creativity and problem-solving skills to merge together. Change your view and your focus will follow.

There are many ways to change the scenery.

- ♥ Take a walk or drive and clear your mind
- ♥ Hang a new picture
- ♥ Rearrange the furniture
- ♥ Work in a different room
- ♥ Work from the coffee shop, library, or a park bench

Any of these ideas can assist in refocusing your outlook by changing your surroundings.

Changing scenery helps clear your mind and gives you the opportunity to reframe your focus. This allows you to focus in a more positive, creative direction. You will be ready to attend any situation. Inspiration and creativity are born out of risk taking and challenging yourself. Remember Happy first, situation second.

Things change. Let yourself flow with ease through the many changes life will bring your way. Accept change. Instigate change. Take delight in change. Learn to embrace change. Change is growth, so don't be afraid or hesitant. Welcome the unseen gifts change brings.

Create your Vibration Card now.

MORE
Change!

~ 25 ~
Create Positive Affirmations

Start your day by writing down a positive affirmation. When you connect to a positive affirmation, you make it a real part of your day. You internalize it, commit to it, and own it! Write something new from your heart and write often.

Make writing a positive affirmation part of your morning routine. Place the affirmation where you will see it often to add focus and determination to your affirmation. Keep a record of your favourite affirmations in your gratitude journal and use them again and again.

Here are twenty of my affirmations to get you started.

- ♥ I am love. I am purpose. I was made with divine intention.
- ♥ I am adventurous. I overcome fears by following my dreams.
- ♥ I am in charge of how I feel and today I am choosing happiness.
- ♥ I have the power to create change.
- ♥ I let go of everything that no longer serves me.
- ♥ I can do anything.
- ♥ I am unstoppable.
- ♥ I experience love wherever I go. Loving people fill my life, and I find myself easily expressing love to others.
- ♥ I am in tune with the Universe and it guides me effortlessly.
- ♥ My day begins and ends with gratitude and joy.
- ♥ Today is going to be a really, really, really GREAT day!
- ♥ Life supports me in every possible way.
- ♥ I am a unique and beautiful soul.
- ♥ I am open to new and wonderful changes.
- ♥ All areas of my life are abundant and fulfilling.
- ♥ My mind and body are in perfect balance.
- ♥ I feel glorious, dynamic energy.
- ♥ My confidence knows no limits.
- ♥ I am worthy of love and joy.
- ♥ I choose to be happy every day.

Affirmations are declarations that serve to maintain your focus, creativity and positive energy. Commit to daily affirmations and you will see positive changes in your life that will build and support your happiness.

You are worthy. You were born worthy.
You do not need to prove your worthiness nor must you earn it.
All you have to do is connect with it and enjoy it.

Create your Vibration Card now.

MORE
Affirmations!

~ 26 ~
Start a Hobby

Do you already have a hobby? Can you expand on it, or are you ready to start something new? Anything you are interested in can become a hobby.

- ♥ Start a collection
- ♥ Take music lessons
- ♥ Sign up for a craft evening
- ♥ Join an established group (model trains, cabinetry, baking, wine tasting)
- ♥ Learn another language
- ♥ Grow something green

Hobbies are outlets for happy focus and creativity. They provide a safe, non-judgemental place for your mind to rest against in times of joy or angst. Rest from a busy life. Enjoy a relaxing exploration of something you are interested in, just for fun.

My oldest daughter decided to write a book and has now written and published three books through her own publishing company. She also runs a very successful bed & breakfast.

In her mid-thirties, my youngest daughter decided to take voice lessons. This hobby morphed into guitar lessons. We attend her recitals twice a year.

When I turned 40, I started collecting bears. It turned into quite the focus for many years. As a result, I have a house full of bears; many have found homes with the grandchildren but most are still here with me. They offer a bit of joy every time I look at them, and I have them in every room.

There are creative outlets all around you. Look to your community associations for short and long term courses. There are many ways to explore your creativity without committing; a painting class at a pub or a drop-in dance class. Be adventurous enough to try something once. Investigate several until you find one that inspires your creativity. Creativity feeds the soul. It doesn't have to be expensive, but it must be fun and preferably non-competitive.

Creativity brings joy to the heart.
Spend time exploring your creative nature.
Find something that soothes the soul and jump in!

Create your Vibration Card now.

MORE
Creativity!

～ 27 ～
Imagine a Perfect Moment

This exercise takes only a few minutes, so make yourself comfortable in a quiet place where you will not be disturbed. Once you are comfortable, close your eyes, take in a slow, deep breath, hold it, count to three and exhale slowly. Imagine what a perfect moment would look like in your life right now?

- ♥ Where are you?
- ♥ What are doing?
- ♥ What are the details of the moment?
- ♥ What are you wearing?
- ♥ What is the weather?
- ♥ Who is with you?
- ♥ What can you smell?
- ♥ What can you hear?
- ♥ How do you feel?

Engage in a variety of feelings that you experience in the perfect moment. Imagine it so clearly that you can almost feel your reality shift. Let the positive energy of the perfect moment wash over you and through you. Savor it, imprint it in your mind and gather all the positive energy you can from your vision. Take a few more cleansing breaths and go back to your day.

As you practice this exercise it will become easier to create perfect moments. You may be surprised at how quickly this exercise can help you shift from ho-hum to Happy!

If you find yourself in a very anxious moment, excuse yourself and find a quiet place to do a mini-meditation of your perfect moment and rebalance your energy. You will be more productive and your positive energy will help those around you.

Moments fill us with joy and happiness.
Waiting for the perfect moment may take too long —
create your happy moments yourself and enjoy!

Create your Vibration Card now.

MORE Moments!

~ 28 ~
Soak in a Hot Bath

There is nothing like a long soak in a hot bath or shower (I prefer a jetted tub, but any tub will do). A hot bath is an excellent way to make time for a little self-care and reflection each day. Hot water soothes and relaxes your entire body and mind. Add some comforting essential oils, put on some soft music, light a few candles, pour yourself a glass of wine and create a perfect oasis. This is a great way to rid your system of negative energy from the day and rejuvenate and realign your positive energy.

If you experience many conflicting emotions, you can choose to put Happy first. Events that bring conflict and challenge will always be part of life. You can choose to be happy first as you deal with the situations to keep yourself in a positive mindframe. It is exhausting to swing from positive energy to negative energy all day long. At the end of the day, it doesn't matter what happens, you can choose to be happy or unhappy; so why not choose Happy! It is empowering to know *you are in control* and you can decide. "At the end of the day, It's the end of the day".

Use your spa time to reflect on and evaluate your day. Ease your mind and adjust any emotional remnants left from the day with intention and determination. Practice some breathing and meditation techniques and soak in the happiness.

You are important. It is your primary job to take care of you. Put self-care at the top of your to-do list. You matter!

Create your Vibration Card now.

MORE
Self-Care!

∼ 29 ∼
Grab Your Power

This exercise was gleaned from Marshall Sylver[9], famed hypnotist, creator of the *Turning Point* seminars and author of *Passion, Profit and Power.*

Stand up tall. Make a fist with your dominant hand. With your fisted hand, push straight up into the air, three times, as you say the mantra below out loud. Say it with passion, vigor, and commitment!

Power! POWER! POWER!

Did you feel the energy surging through you? If not, do it again, with MORE emotion! Engaging with personal power feels great and leads to increased confidence. Often, individuals give away their personal power and disconnect from passion. This is not a Happy feeling.

One way to recover from this is to stand tall and take back your power. Grab it! It is your power, so welcome power back into your heart, mind, and spirit. When you sit in a position of personal power and connect to your passions, you will feel strong, vibrant and happy.

To paraphrase a beautiful Cherokee Story:
We have two wolves at battle within us.
One is angry, sad, and fearful. The other is joyful,
peaceful and kind. Which wolf will win the battle?

The one you feed.

Create your Vibration Card now.

MORE
Power!

~ 30 ~
Install Happy Buttons

Don and I were grandparenting our three granddaughters for a week. The oldest was not having a good day. She was about nine years old and nothing I said or did was helping; she was not a happy child.

I asked, "What if we install a Happy Button right here?" as I pointed to the area just below her collar bone on the left side, "And what if we install another one here?" as I pointed to her right side "And then we pushed the buttons and it made you feel Happy!" At that moment, I caught a little smirk. It was very little, but it was progress, and I capitalized on it. Success was in our near future and a smile was forming inside and was working its way outside to face the world again.

The picture below is the result of that conversation. I found it on the counter in the morning, a gift to Grandma. To this day, it has a prominent place in my office.

Happy Buttons — where will you install yours? Above your heart? Inside your wrist? Install a couple as a simple reminder that happiness is always a choice. If you find yourself feeling down, discouraged, or anxious, press on the area where you imagine your happy button to be. Breathe in and let happiness fill you up!

Regardless of the situation you find yourself in, you can always choose to be happy. Situations don't define you; they come and go. Happiness can be with you throughout your life if you choose it. Let your life be defined by the joy you feel each day.

Create your Vibration Card now.

MORE Happiness!

Closing Notes

The secret to happiness is simple, and it isn't really a secret.

First, *recognize* how you are feeling, and *allow* that feeling. Be with it and accept it. Explore it a little. Where do you feel it? Can you give it a name? Is it heavy? Is it dark? Can you identify the source of it? It's just a feeling — it's not likely to harm you. It's fine to sit with it, whether it is good, or not so good. However, once you've explored a negative feeling for a little while, it's time to shift to something that feels better. And this is where choice comes in. It is now up to you to *decide* to do whatever you need to do to improve how you are feeling and to do it *immediately*.

I read once that it's ok to wallow in negative feelings like sadness, anger, or fear . . . just don't do it for too long. Recognize if you are beginning to feel sorry for yourself, as this is not productive. A strong indicator that you have become preoccupied with negative feelings is your self-talk. If your self-talk is labeling you and shaming you, then you have been in the negative cycle for too long; its time to get out! Reaching this point, and choosing to change my self-talk has helped me many times when things don't go quite the way I planned. When that old familiar "why me" or "I'm so stupid" crop up it's like a little buzzer going off ... and I know it's time to make a shift and think better, more positive thoughts!

Sometimes it's hard to think better thoughts, yet I know that the sooner I become proactive and shift my thoughts just a little, the better off I am. Little thoughts that feel better add up to feeling more positive, and that is the pathway to future success and balance!

Happiness is a choice, so always choose thoughts that propel you towards joy and happiness. I truly believe that our purpose in life is to experience more joy, more love, and more *happiness*. We defy our purpose when we dwell in the negative.

The activities I share in the book are designed to help you move to a higher level of vibration, to feel happier, and to think thoughts on purpose, one thought at a time.

Does it work? Absolutely, it works 100% of the time, every time. Give the process time. It took years to get into the negative energy ruts, so be easy on yourself and give yourself time to learn new routines that will pull you out of those ruts.

The secret of success is recognizing where you are, *deciding* to think positive thoughts, and doing whatever you need to do to move in the direction of happiness.

My hope is that you will discover new ways to think happy, positive thoughts and that you will decide to *think on purpose* so that your journey through life moves you ever closer to true happiness.

I truly hope that you enjoy this journey, and that it brings you many brilliant discoveries. Wishing you *happiness* at every turn.

Janet Legere

Acknowledgements

There have been many people who have influenced my life. Some were good. Some were bad. All left their mark and helped me discover my happy self.

It doesn't matter what kind of influence someone has had in your life. Your happiness is your job regardless of what or who is going on in your life. Happiness is a *choice*.

My husband Don is my true champion. He has been by my side since the day we met, supporting me, loving me and ALWAYS making me laugh. Together, we discovered a joy that can only be experienced when you let happiness in.

My children are the light of my life. My two daughters, Tina and Brenda, have been my anchors. In 2008, we started meeting for lunch every week, and to this day we make the effort to continue our tradition. My girls have allowed me into the inner beings of their souls and together we started solving all the problems in our lives, one Wednesday at a time. My son, Danial, always makes me laugh and we have a special bond that only a mother and son can experience.

My step-daughters, Sydney, Kassandra, and Maggie all have giving hearts and loving personalities. I love them as though they were my own children and they have become dear friends who have secured a special place in my heart.

My grandchildren have shown me the true meaning of happiness. It has been, and continues to be, an absolute honor to influence these special little beings. How proud they make me.

There are many friends who have come into my life, and each has left their mark. They are so special to me, and too numerous to list all of them here. I hope I have left a bit of me with each of them. I do want to make mention of three very special women who have loved me and supported me all my life. My best friends since elementary school and high school are Grace, Carol & Margaret. They never judged me and always had much sagely advice to offer. They have supported my crazy ideas and always allowed me to bring happiness into their lives.

I also want to mention one very special friend, Pam. Without her, this book would not have been written. We journeyed together to discover our truths and heal. Along the way she never judged and was always lovingly supportive. We helped each other learn how to enjoy happiness!

Another individual who was an enormous influence on my life is Devlyn Steele. He was my first 'mentor' and coach. He showed me how to get my life back and many of the activities in this book are as a result of Devlyn's program, *Tools To Life*. Devlyn was the first person to show me a plan that would help me create any life I wanted. He helped me 'retrain' my brain and let go of everything that didn't serve me. He has been instrumental in helping me create the life I am living.

And last, but certainly not least, there is my Mom. Although she left this world when I was just 25, she influenced me to be the best that I can be. She was a powerful woman who left a lasting impression on everyone she met.

I acknowledge and thank everyone who has touched my life. Thank you for what you brought, what you left, and what became of the *Janet* you influenced.

References

1. Devlyn Steele, *Tools To Life* | Crunchbase, Retrieved 2019.
    Https://www.crunchbase.com/organization/tools-to-life

2. Janet Legere, The Morning Motivator, Retrieved 2019.
    http://the-morning-motivator.com/, 2019

3. Lee Jampolsky, *Smile For No Good Reason*, 2015.

4. Robert W. Coleman Elementary School, Retrieved 2019
    https://www.cnn.com/2016/11/04/health/
    meditation-in-schools-baltimore/index.html

    https://www.washingtonpost.com/local/education/
    how-mindfulness-practices-are-changing-an-inner-city-
    school/2016/11/13/7b4a274a-a833-11e6-ba59-a7d93165c6d4_
    story.html?noredirect=on&utm_term=.8a63066669dc

5. Esther and Jerry Hicks, *Ask and It Will Be Given Learning To
    Manifest Your Desires*, Hay House, Inc. 2004.

6. Lori Granger, Let It Go, https://youtu.be/1CDZGXlHYp8
    Retrieved 2019.

7. Carolyn Diamond, 10 Carat Diamond, Released 1985.
    https://youtu.be/lI7JzSW7PJO . Retrieved 2019.

8. Pam Grout, *E-squared*, Hay House, Inc. 2013.

9. Marshall Sylver, *Passion, Profit and Power*, Simon and Schuster, 1995.

About the Author

Janet Legere is a wife, mother, grandmother, sister, aunt, and friend to many. She has a passion for life and a mission to empower others to be their very best.

Janet has been a full-time Internet Marketer and Coach for 20 years, sharing her skills and gifts in the global arena. She infuses her strategies for joy and happiness into all of her training, making every step a simple, accessible, and positive learning experience.

Check out the **Be That Books** Series!

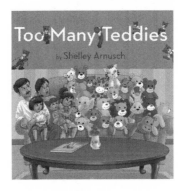

Made in the USA
Middletown, DE
16 December 2020